MAP
OF THE
SOUL:
EGO
I AM

MURRAY STEIN
with
Steven Buser & Leonard Cruz

 CHIRON PUBLICATIONS • ASHEVILLE, N.C.

To BTS and their ARMY of fans

www.ChironPublications.com

Interior design by Danijela Mijailovic
Cover design by Claudia Sperl
Printed primarily in the United States of America.

ISBN 978-1-63051-841-7 paperback
ISBN 978-1-63051-842-4 hardcover
ISBN 978-1-63051-843-1 electronic
ISBN 978-1-63051-844-8 limited edition paperback

Library of Congress Cataloging-in-Publication Data

Names: Stein, Murray, 1943- author. | Buser, Steven, 1963- author. | Cruz, Leonard, 1957- author.
Title: Map of the soul-ego : I am / Murray Stein ; with Steven Buser & Leonard Cruz.
Description: Asheville, N.C. : Chiron Publications, [2020] | Series: Map of the soul series ; volume 3 | Includes bibliographical references. | Summary: "In Map of the Soul - Ego: I Am, Dr. Murray Stein explores the beginnings of consciousness and the concept of the "I," as well as the evocative lyrics from the Korean Pop band BTS's album, Map of the Soul: 7. BTS's album series titled Map of the Soul was largely inspired by Dr. Stein's presentation of C.G. Jung's groundbreaking psychological insights. Ego is the center of consciousness. Yet, "ego can separate itself from the body, and then become a virtual reality in its own right." This book is an overview of the ego from a Jungian perspective but also is a rich and nuanced examination of how the creative spark can ignite and sustain meaningful psychological growth. The author and collaborators are deeply indebted to BTS, whose world-wide popularity points to their remarkable ability to tap into universal themes. BTS's music in-spired this work and this introductory series of books may inspire others to explore their inner life"— Provided by publisher.
Identifiers: LCCN 2020021910 (print) | LCCN 2020021911 (ebook) | ISBN 9781630518417 (v. 3 ; paperback) | ISBN 9781630518424 (v. 3 ; hardcover) | ISBN 9781630518448 (v. 3 ; limited edition paperback) | ISBN 9781630518431 (v. 3 ; ebook)
Subjects: LCSH: Ego (Psychology) | Consciousness. | BTS (Musical group)
Classification: LCC BF175.5.E35 S74 2020 (print) | LCC BF175.5.E35 (ebook) | DDC 155.2—dc23
LC record available at https://lccn.loc.gov/2020021910
LC ebook record available at https://lccn.loc.gov/2020021911

Special thanks to *BTS ARMY,*
Carla at the *ARMY Help Center,*
Laura London at *Speaking of Jung*
and to BTS for bringing Jungian
psychology to a new generation.

Table of Contents

Introduction to
Map of the Soul: Ego
By Murray Stein

A description of the psyche can begin at any number of points. In previous books we have taken a survey of the persona (*Map of the Soul: Persona*) and the shadow (*Map of the Soul: Shadow*), which consist of our social identities and our hidden motivations. If we think of the psyche as a house, the persona is the front facade, which faces the street and projects what real estate agents call "curb appeal." It is our self-presentation to the collective world around us. The shadow is a character who lives in the basement, a part of the personality that is hidden from the world outside and even from the inhabitants who live on the floors of the house aboveground.

The present book is about the ego (*Map of the Soul: Ego*). The ego is the character who is called "I" and occupies the ground and first floors of the house.

"I" thinks it is in control of the house and plays the role of "the boss." It is the focal figure, the protagonist in the story, and feels entitled to the claim of ownership of the house. All the other characters who live in house with the ego are there because they are connected or related to the ego in one way or another. They make up what we call the contents of consciousness, and they are there in full view and behave as though they are under the ego's control, even if often they are not as controlled as they seem. They are the close relatives and are more or less well known, unlike the shadow who lives in the basement. The ego is somewhat aware of the persona but less aware of the shadow. Both are on the fringes of consciousness, and the ego does not pay much attention to them unless there are problems.

I will speak of the ego as "I" or "it" in order to avoid attribution of gender. With respect to the ego, there is essentially no difference between men and women, as we shall see. As far as this agency is concerned, the genders are equal. The owner of the house may be "she" or "he," and therefore in order to avoid any bias one way or the other I will speak of ego without reference to gender.

The ego is also what we call our "will." The fuel of the psyche is "energy" (sometimes called "libido" in Jungian circles but without reference to sexuality), and the ego has a certain amount of free energy at its disposal. To an extent, it can choose what it wants to do with the house—let's say the color of the walls, the pictures hanging on them and commemorating the ancestors, and the other objects that have been collected and remembered over time. The ego has some power to change these aspects of the house, if it wills to do so, and to make decisions that can introduce alterations large and small. It can change its surroundings and relationships to a large extent but not totally. Often the ego believes it has more freedom to make decisions than it actually possesses. This is a common illusion and probably necessary for the sake of self-confidence and self-esteem.

The ego does have some specific qualities in the individual, a type of character surrounding the neutral core. This character is sometimes described in typological terms: a tendency toward introversion or extroversion, toward thinking or feeling, toward sensation or intuition. The character style of the ego can be discovered by taking type inventory tests like the Myers-Briggs Type Inventory (MBTI) or Gifts Compass (GC). Both are available online and can help people take a look at their ego typology in an objective fashion.

To discover the core of the ego, however, it is necessary to introspect deeply, to look in the mirror, not at the dressed-up persona but at the naked person. If you ask yourself, for instance, "What is it in me that thinks this thought or feels this feeling?"

and take a careful look at that part of yourself, you will begin to get a sense of the essential ego. It is a still small center of consciousness.

The ego tends to become intimately identified with its surroundings and with certain values and words, like a name. Here is an exercise: Try to separate your "I" from your given name (Jane or John) and your family name (Smith or Jones), then from your neighborhood and city and country, from memories good and bad. As you peel away these identities, you will be left with the essence of what the ego is: pure self-consciousness. It's a central point of reflexive consciousness. The ego is the center of consciousness.

While the ego is identified with many things such as given and family names, nationality, gender, race, etc., it is identified to an even larger extent with the physical body. Actually, the ego is an intimate aspect of the body it occupies. It is the body's center of consciousness, and it makes it possible for that body to become aware of itself as separate and independent and to take care of itself. This makes the body aware of its individuality and uniqueness. The ego is the "I" of the body, and every human body has one.

A client recently said something to me that puzzled me at first. She had recently suffered from a minor illness and told me: "My body knew I was sick before I did." She was referring to some physical symptoms that had gone unnoticed but could have given her ego a clue of the coming illness. She also had some dreams that in retrospect indicated the coming illness. Here she was using the word "I" in two different senses: first, as a part of the body ("my body knew I was sick") as though "I" and the body are one; second, as separate from the body (before "I" did") as though "I" and the body are two. The first refers to the body as "I," and the second refers to the ego as "I." The two "I's" are different but also the same. This is a paradox of the human psyche. The ego can separate itself from the body, and then it becomes a virtual reality in its own right.

We spontaneously make this distinction/confusion all the time without noticing it. And we can do this because the ego is *self-conscious*, that is, it is conscious of itself as a distinct psychic entity and separate from the body or anything other in the environment. The philosopher René Descartes made the famous statement as he was developing his theory of knowledge, "I think therefore I am." Here he is separating his "I" from the rest of his body and the world around him and identifying it with his cognitive function. But the "I" can also be separated from thinking, as he implicitly does when he says, "I think." What is the "I" that is doing the thinking? It is not the thought or the function of thinking. It is separate even from such inner activities as thinking and feeling.

Many philosophies question the reality of the ego. Does the ego really exist, or is it nothing more than a product of reflection, like an image in a mirror. An object seen in a mirror is not real, it is only virtual. It is a kind of illusion. But then, we may ask, what about the mirror? Is the mirror real? Not the image in the mirror (our "identity"), but the mirror itself? Something in us is doing the mirroring.

In truth, the ego is the mirror and not the contents in the mirror. The contents in the mirror are the contents of consciousness and separate from the ego just as the images in a mirror are separate from the mirror. The mirror (the "I") has psychic reality, similar to the other aspects of the psyche such as shadow and persona and the contents of the personal and collective unconscious. Now, if we step back for a moment and reflect on the mirror itself, we ask a still deeper question: What is it that is now doing the reflecting? It is a reflection on reflection itself, one mirror looking at another mirror. We are in a hall of mirrors. And this is still the ego. It is the ego reflecting on itself until it becomes so purified that no contents remain, only a pure reflective surface.

The ego is the center of whatever consciousness we might have or be able to develop. If there is consciousness of any kind, there must be an ego to register it. This was Jung's argument in contrast to the philosophies that deny the ego's reality. As long as there is consciousness, there is also this psychic factor called the ego. No matter what is being experienced, even "the void" itself as Zen Buddhism speaks of it, the ego is there as the recorder of it, as the "I" that is having the experience. In a sense, the "I" and the experience are one (as phenomenology has it), and in a sense they are not but are rather more like a mirror and the images reflected in it. They are hard to separate, but in truth they are two aspects of an experience.

Sometimes the ego is front and center, as when we say: "I want," "I will," "I can." But sometimes it is in the background as a witness to what is happening. If we feel a strong emotion, we may become totally identified with it, as when we say, "I am sad" or "I am afraid." Or we remain apart as when we say: "I am feeling sadness" or "I am filled with anxiety." The one statement shows the ego as the central character in the story; the other shows the ego as witness to an event. A strong ego can do both. It can assert, "I will!" and take action, and it can contain thoughts, feelings, and fantasies without acting on them or identifying totally with them. When we speak of a strong ego, we mean that it can act and it can contain. (As an aside, the ego that is represented in the musical album *Map of the Soul: 7* by BTS is a strong ego: able to suffer and able to act.)

The ego has to deal with both inner and outer realities that lie beyond its control. When we speak of inner realities, we are talking about powerful emotions, memories positive and negative (even traumatic), fascinating and horrifying ideas, alluring and grotesque fantasies, pulsating impulses and so forth. Sometimes we speak of "complexes," which are autonomous energies of the inner world that can have a huge impact on how the ego feels and behaves. Or we reference "instincts," which are powerful drives urging us to act immediately in order to satisfy their urgent cravings and desires. The ego has to manage these inner forces and try to balance their demands with other pressures that come from the world without. The instinct may say: "Eat! Now!" But the ego may have to say: "Wait! It's not time to eat right now." The ego is sometimes successful in moderating the demands of the inner world, and sometimes it is not and acts out. The same holds for demands made by the outer world. The ego must respond to them and weigh them against other considerations like values, integrity, ambition, and so forth.

The ego is responsible for our sense of reality inner and outer, and as such, it confronts the demands of fantasy and drive within and social and political messages from without. Time is a crucial factor in the reality of the material world around us. The ego has to take note of this factor and balance the demands of desire and reality. Sometimes this creates painful frustrations and conflicts. It is a feature of a strong ego that it can bear a lot of frustration and can hold the tension of opposites.

Jung takes note of five instincts: hunger, sexual desire, the urges to be active and to reflect, and creativity. The first two are familiar as instinctual forces in human nature, a part of physical existence and survival, and they cause a lot of problems if they are not well managed by the ego. The need to be physically active and in motion is partially physically based and partially psychological. The urge to be active is very strong and can run out of control. It becomes an addiction when it can no longer be modulated by the ego. Sometimes the muscles scream for action, and only a strong ego can say: "It's midnight. This is not the time for running in the park." The other two—reflection and creativity—are not generally thought of as instincts because they are not as directly based in physiological processes, but it is useful to think of them in this way because they also make powerful and sometimes almost irresistible demands on the ego. The instinct for reflection can drive people to excess and exhaustion. It is the source of high culture on the one hand, but it can also become a destructive tyrant on the other. And people with a strong instinct for creativity will testify that this "daimon" can take control of the ego and drive it to extremes that are not healthy. The ego can become possessed by the energies of the instincts and thus lose control of the household it is supposed to be managing.

The ego needs to be strong in order to manage the forces that make their claims. Like a muscle, it gains strength by pushing back against resistances. I learned about this type of muscle building by watching a college classmate doing isometric exercises. He was a powerfully built athlete and would stand in the doorway to his room pushing on both sides with his arms for minutes at a time. He was building his arm muscles by pushing as hard as he could against immovable objects. For some people, studying a subject like mathematics is like doing isometric exercises and has the same effect on their ego strength: It is a totally impossible task, but by staying with the frustrations and holding the tension, they are building their capacity for dealing with psychological frustrations and conflicts that will inevitably arise in life. Jung once said that the really important problems in life cannot be solved, they can only be outgrown. The ego may not only survive the struggles but grow in strength from them. Dealing with frustration is a path to ego-building.

At the extreme, one thinks of the figure of Job in the Bible. God allows Satan to arrange things so he will lose everything he has, only not his life. He suffers the maximum degree of loss—children, wealth, reputation—and he is left to his own devices without assistance from his wife or so-called friends. But he has the fortitude to hold out despite all the frustration dealt him by his friends and the devastation delivered by Satan, and finally in a tremendous vision, he gains knowledge of the Divine and manages to outlive his personal catastrophe. Indeed, in the end he is blessed with more than he had at the beginning of the story.

Many folk tales and fairy tales tell a similar story. The character who can endure the tests and trials in the end wins the prize. This is the outcome not especially for the clever but for the resilient. Resilience is a quality in the ego much to be prized. It should be a primary goal of the ego's education and development. (The final song of BTS's album *Map of the Soul: 7*, titled "ON," expresses and celebrates this virtue impressively.)

BTS and *Outro: Ego*
By Murray Stein

*This chapter is adapted from an interview
with Murray Stein conducted by Laura London
on the podcast Speaking of Jung: Interviews
with Jungian Analysts Episode #54.*

Outro: Ego is one of the songs and videos from
BTS' Map of The Soul: 7 and was released in February
2020. This album continues BTS's exploration of the
Map of the Soul concept from Carl Jung and focuses
particularly on ego and shadow. The song *Outro: Ego*
circles around the psychological concept of the "I,"
the center of the conscious personality.

Ego

Our psychological understanding of "ego"
differs from what it means in common usage and
everyday life. In psychology, it is a technical term,

while in casual conversation we often speak of "ego" in judgmental or moralistic terms. It has a negative spin when we say that people have "too much ego" or "a big ego." This judges them as too self-centered and narcissistic. In psychology, however, the term "ego" has a different meaning. It is the center of consciousness. Ego is Latin for "I." The "I" can be self-centered, or it can be altruistic. It can be colored by a multitude of different attitudes. In itself, however, it is neutral, like a dot of light in a field of dark objects.

In psychology, we speak of the ego as the center of consciousness. This indicates its location. It occupies a central place in that part of the psyche that is conscious. As we know, the psyche is much larger than consciousness. In fact, consciousness is a rather small part of the psyche, even though we often think of it as the totality because it is what we are aware of. The contents of consciousness are in the field of consciousness because they are closely connected to the ego. Otherwise, they would drift away and be lost in the unconscious. The contents are feelings, memories, images, thoughts, etc. The ego is like a magnet and holds them in consciousness until they fade and fall away. That's what we call forgetting or repressing.

Jung sometimes uses the metaphor of a light in the darkness to describe what he means by ego. Imagine that you're walking in a forest at night and you can't see anything. It's totally dark around you. Then you light a match and use the match to light a candle. Now you can see a few things around you. You become aware of what's out there. The ego is like that: It is a light in the darkness of the unconscious psyche. Without an ego, we couldn't see anything in the darkness, especially of the inner world. We could not keep memories or feelings or thoughts in place. They would disappear as soon as they became manifest. The ego lights things up and allows you to see them more clearly and to keep them in your awareness. If you have a strong flashlight, you can see even further into the darkness of the forest around you. You can see trees and animals. You can differentiate your surroundings and orient yourself in your world. If you have a strong ego, you can see deeper into the inner world and the hidden aspects of the outer world. Your ability to perceive and to differentiate depends on the light supplied by the ego.

Ego is also very much related to our sense of body, of being in our body and one with this material object in the world. If something happens to the body, the ego suffers, whether it's a blow to the head or an illness to the lungs or whatever. The ego identifies with the specific body that you are. If you are ill, your ego strength is diminished, and you can't function as well in your consciousness. You can't think as clearly and might get confused. Sometimes the ego breaks free of the body as in what are called "out-of-body" experiences or in certain moments of meditation. Generally, though, ego consciousness and the body are intimately connected. "I and the body are one" might be a way to say it.

However, in consciousness we can roam around in the world as well. We can travel through time, as when we study history or read novels; we can live in alternative realities as when we create fictions or watch movies; we can enter into highly abstract worlds as when we study mathematics or quantum physics. When we are in love, our ego becomes one with another person. Think of ego basically as the center of consciousness, and wherever consciousness goes, the ego remains at its center. It's like the driver of the car that can travel far and over many terrains. What you do in your consciousness is ego-directed, unless the ego falls under the control of other parts of the personality, such as complexes and archetypal figures. Then the driver of the car is not the ego. The ego is in the passenger seat and sometimes uncomfortably so. Your ego has a fair amount of free will to make decisions, what you want to do, what you want to eat, what you want to wear, and so on. The ego is involved in decision making. But it is not totally free of the influences of inner and outer forces.

The persona is a mask we wear to adapt to the world around us, to function in the world. The ego is behind that, so to speak. It's the person behind the mask. The shadow is the contrary to the persona and also has a powerful influence on the ego. Sometimes the ego is caught in the conflict between what the persona demands and what the shadow desires. This is often the cause of neurosis and psychological suffering.

Outro: Ego

Outro is typically a concluding section of music, but we don't really know what *outro* means in this song. Does it mean it's the end of the whole series that they're going out on this note of ego, or is it going to be only the concluding song of this album? What does this song mean in the lives of BTS? What are they saying about themselves? I consider BTS as a single personality of sorts. Even though the songs are sung by individuals, like J-Hope and Suga and so on, they're also singing for the group. BTS is getting older. The members aren't boys anymore. They started as a boys group. The K-Pop groups are usually very young adolescents, teenagers, but these BTS performers are now in their mid-20s. They're reaching another stage of life and they're becoming adults. They'll soon be hitting midlife in their 30s. This coming to oneself as an ego is a part of that process in the first half of life.

Outro: Ego, celebrates the moment when we realize "I am I." I am not you; I am not some other; I am I. Jung had this experience and records it in his autobiography, *Memories, Dreams, Reflections*. He said it was like stepping out of a cloud, and suddenly he realized: I am I, I am myself. This coming to oneself and affirming one's uniqueness, one's individuality, is the coming of age of the ego. It is an initiation into life as an individual, separate from others. "I am" means "I exist as an I," as one of a kind. The sense of temporality is a strong part of this song, the sense of time passing. I'm here for only a short period of time in the history of the planet. This is ego awareness, the reality of time and finitude. This song is an *outro* in the sense of BTS finishing one stage of life and taking up the next. This is all part of the individuation of the members of BTS and of BTS as a group.

Individuation is the term that Jung used to describe psychological development through the lifespan. The lifespan is the entire course of a person's life from the time in the mother's womb until the last breath is given up and the person passes away. That is the lifespan of the individual. What happens psychologically and developmentally within that lifespan is what Jung called individuation. Individuation ultimately means becoming the individual that you are born to be. You are born with a certain code, a genetic code, but also a psychological code, which underlies the emergence of your potentials and development of talents and abilities.

Time Rushes Ever Forward

In *Outro: Ego* J-Hope sings "time rushes ever forward" and about "choices by my fate." He speaks of memories of when he was a child, and in the video there's a photograph of him as a young boy. This has to do with the realization that the important decisions we make in life determine our life course with some finality. When you're young, you think, well, there are so many different directions you could take, so many things you could do. Maybe you'll try one thing for a while, and if it doesn't work out, you'll try something else for a while. The consequences of choices are minimized. When you're young, there are vast potentials, and you don't have to settle on anything in particular right away. For BTS members, however, their fate was sealed when they were identified as having this amazing musical performance ability and were taken into training. The decision to go along with that opportunity, whoever made the decision, became their fate and their destiny. That is their life, and it's irreversible. When you get the sense that time flows in only one direction and that is forward, and you also realize it doesn't go backward or stand still, then you're living in the ego. Ego lives with temporality, with the flow of time from past to present to future, one way.

Before the ego is very well developed, time doesn't exist in the same sense. For the infant, time is not a factor; it lives in atemporality, the eternal Now. This is a paradisal state: no time, no death, no aging, no yesterday or tomorrow. As you grow older, you begin to live with a sense of temporality, and you learn to take time seriously into account as you make your decisions. You live in process and in a consequential world where decisions make a difference and there are hard decisions and roads not taken. You cannot return to the past. J-Hope remembers his childhood, and there's nostalgia in the memory. Of course, it's important to remember the past, but you cannot go back there. The realization that you can't go backward into the past and that time does not stand still but moves ever forward is a very important moment. Suddenly, you realize that you have to face the present and the future. It's a turning point in development, when the ego becomes aware of temporality and its consequences. The choices and decisions we make have effects not only in the moment but for the future.

J-Hope is coming to that realization in the song. He sings, "touch of the devil, fateful recall." The devil is shadow, and perhaps a devil was involved in his decision to become a BTS star, the devil of ambition. In the earlier song in the album, *Interlude: Shadow*, Suga sings: "I wanna be a rockstar" and "I wanna be rich." There is the touch of the devil in some of the choices we make; that is, the shadow gets in and pushes us in a certain direction, motivates us to take a certain step, and then we come to the realization that we can't reverse this process that has been set in motion. We look back and we may think, "Wow, I wonder if I really should have done that. Maybe I shouldn't have." But it's too late, and you can't undo it. You can't redo the past; it is done. You have to move forward and grieve the past, or remember it and honor it, but you cannot go back into it.

Ego and Shadow

Jung said it's not healthy to be too good because what you're leaving out is the shadow, which is an essential part of the whole personality. One-sidedness breeds neurosis. So acting out the shadow isn't always a bad thing. Sometimes, of course, it is, and you do terrible things when the shadow bursts out of control and you regret the results and might even go to prison for it. But if you can get hold of the shadow and understand it, you can learn from it. We make mistakes, we do things that are regrettable, but we also thrive by tapping into the energies of the shadow, and it moves us into a new place that we would not have arrived at otherwise. Certainly, you can see that here with J-Hope. He's attained the pinnacle of fame and fortune that he wouldn't have achieved had that devil not nudged him to take the fateful step into becoming a BTS member.

We all like to chase shadows in others. We find the darkness in other people and in the world around us. The idea of taking back our shadow projections is to find that thing that we see as dark or evil or bad in the others and somehow see its true location inside of ourselves. There are a number of ways that we can try to do this. While it's very hard to see behind yourself, maybe a close friend can tell you about your shadow. Or you might have a dream in which shadow figures appear and you work with those dream images to understand them more. We do a lot of work in psychoanalysis to try to get close to the shadow and discover its meaning. As analysts, we try not to humiliate or embarrass people or to make them feel guilty, but rather to see more clearly their role and responsibility within their relationships. People who are without shadow awareness tend to constantly be victims and blame everybody else for their problems. The world is bad, they're innocent; they're good, the world around them is at fault. It's very hard to break through that kind of a mentality because it's invested in not feeling guilty. When you touch shadow, you feel a little guilt, you feel some shame, but that shouldn't stop you from acknowledging your shadow. If you know it's there and accept it, it's easier to prevent it from repeating the same response over and over again.

Suffering and Ego Strength

It's in the struggles that we learn the most about ourselves. When we reflect back on our lives, we don't think so much about the smooth sailing times, but rather the moments of struggle or wounding. Those are the ones that we learn the most from, especially the suffering we are responsible for. If you don't struggle to make a decision, you're leaving something undone. You're doing it too easily. We learn from struggling with hard decisions, decisions like getting married, getting divorced, having a child, starting out on a career path, and so on.

A weak ego can't bear very much suffering. A strong ego can bear a lot of suffering. A strong ego can endure hardships and make its way through tough times. A weak ego will collapse, will give up, will withdraw from the world and go into hiding. When I think about people who have a strong ego, I think of someone like Viktor Frankl. During World War II, Frankl was imprisoned in Auschwitz, the notorious Nazi death camp. He survived the horrors of the concentration camp because he had a purpose and he felt his life had meaning. He went on to write his famous book, *Man's Search for Meaning*. He stresses in the book how important a sense of meaning is to make it through difficult events. Meaning is a very important factor in developing a strong ego. If you have a sense of meaning, you can endure a lot of pain and hardship in order to survive. BTS likely experiences a sense of meaning through success and fame, but that, of course, at some point in the future will fade away. Meaning changes. What gives your life meaning now changes over time.

BTS's *Black Swan*

BTS has released another song, titled *Black Swan*, exploring the ego states of despair. The group sings about the dreadful disappearance of meaning. The song was first released via a video of a professional dance company performing to BTS's *Black Swan*. The video opens with a quote from Martha Graham, "A dancer dies twice—once when they stop dancing, and this first death is the more painful."

A dancer often lives for dancing, and dancing can become the essential meaning of that dancer's life. Dancers, like the BTS performers, put everything into their work, into their professional vocation. When dancers' bodies gives out, which often happens relatively early in their lives, their life's meaning suddenly evaporates. BTS is anticipating this moment, when the group will inevitably fall apart and the members will stop performing. This will be their first death and the most painful of deaths. The second death, of course, will be their physical death. The song is a realization that things will end. One's successful moments in the spotlight will come to an end. The light will go out, and you'll be alone, you'll be without the audience, without the applause. It's a very difficult feeling to come to terms with. You feel the anguish in the dancers.

In the *Black Swan* video, you can see the struggles of the white swan trying to fly and the black ones surrounding it and holding it back. It's moving but without success because it can't fly, and it's being crushed by the black swans surrounding it. That's how moods affect us when we fall into a depression or our life loses its meaning. This can happen to anybody and in many different ways. A loved one dies, or you have an accident and you can't do anymore what you could before, you have a stroke, you lose your job. There are many ways you can experience that moment in life. It's not the end of life, though. Those ballet dancers can find another career, perhaps teaching ballet or writing a book about ballet or doing something else in relation to that. But it is a moment of darkness that is very challenging to overcome. The resilient ego can cope with it and move on.

Chasing a Ghost

In *Outro: Ego* J-Hope sings:
"It must have been full of regret with no hope till I die,

With my dance chasing a ghost,
With me blaming my dream
And casting doubt on why I live and breathe
Oh my God God God God
Time goes by
The worries of 7 years finally come out of my
mouth
All the oppressions get resolved

It's a moment of deep reflection in the song. "Chasing a ghost" is chasing something that is very ephemeral, which either doesn't exist or is beyond what we can grasp. He is expressing regret that he has been chasing something ephemeral like a mirage. It's a realization that his ego has been suffering from the pursuit of projections. We project all kinds of things onto the world and onto other people. Then we realize that there's nothing there, or what we thought was there isn't what we thought it would be—it's a mirage. It's a moment of realization and, again, of coming to yourself. A way to strengthen the ego is to look past the projections, to reel them in, and to clean your windshield so that you can see more clearly what's actually around you and what's out there. As long as you're projecting, you're not relating to reality as it is.

Affirming the Ego

Later in *Outro: Ego,* J-Hope's face is super-imposed on paintings of ancient gods. There can be a danger of inflation, since one's celebrity status can feel godlike. When the ego comes into this level of fame and is able to celebrate itself, it can appear godlike to itself and to others. It's a dangerous moment because the ego can exaggerate its capacities and its ability to control life and events. Besides, it's not real and true and will eventually prove to be empty, another mask. The gods are imagined by human beings to live a more or less pain-free life. In most pantheons, the gods are beyond human suffering and beyond the effects of time. They create and they destroy. They have control of time itself. They're very different from the way we experience our lives here in the body as egos. The Greeks talked about hubris, and when humans start thinking that they are gods, they're running the risk of being punished by the gods and struck down. This may come in the form of an illness, an accident, some kind of dire misfortune. In an earlier song, *Interlude: Shadow,* Suga is begging not to fly too high because there's a clear realization that the young person who flies too high will get burned by the sun, will collapse, and will fall to his death. In the song, there's an anxiety about inflation. In *Outro: Ego,* however, the experience of success in the ego is more affirmative. This is a moment in the album of affirming the ego, which can be a beautiful thing. It's in line with the way Jung felt about the ego: The ego is not a bad thing. The ego is our consciousness, it's our awareness, and it's very wrapped up with our individuality. We can affirm the ego. It's a good thing to have a strong ego, just not one that's too inflated.

A Review of the
Map of the Soul
By Steven Buser and Leonard Cruz

The Map

This map of the soul has two center points, the *ego* and the *archetypal Self*. The *archetypal Self* lies at the core of our *ego*. Because this idea is difficult to depict, we have represented it as a cone through which the *ego* funnels into the *archetypal* Self. We will talk more of these structures shortly.

In the upper righthand corner of the map appears a large eye that looks out toward a village or, more accurately, gazes out to the entire world, taking in the totality of what we physically see, hear, smell, and touch. *Ego* perceives reality through the senses. The eye sits atop a range of mountains representing the *persona*. The *persona* is located between the *ego* and the surrounding world since it mediates our presentation to the outside world. Most of the world does not see what lies beyond the *persona*, just as a tall

Persona

Animus

Anima

External
World

Persona

Shadow

Ego

Archetypal
Self

C
A

C
A

C
A

Complex

C
A

C
A

Archetypal
Core of
Complex

Primordial Fire
(deep within collective Unconscious)

mountain range blocks our view of what is beyond. *Persona* is the *mask* we show those around us.

To the far left side of the mountains lies the *shadow* with the *ego* lying midway between. *Shadow* is depicted as a hooded figure. It is no accident that it is found directly opposite to the *persona* on the other side of the mountain range (from the perspective of the *ego*). The *shadow* is the opposite of the *persona*. Whatever positive, acceptable face we show the world through our *persona* is balanced by a darker, unacknowledged, and opposite figure that forms our *shadow*. The *shadow* carries all the unwanted, shameful, unacceptable parts of our psyche. We bury them deep within, hoping they won't be discovered. The *shadow* exists in the unconscious.

In the upper left side of the map, a region that is still in the unconscious realm lie the *anima* and *animus*. These are opposite-gendered, unconscious figures in our soul. The masculine figure is depicted as a warrior, while the feminine figure is dressed in full-length chiton, a type of tunic. The classical Jungian view is that a man possesses a feminine *anima* connecting him to the deeper levels of his unconscious, while a woman possesses a masculine *animus* connecting her to the depths of her unconscious.

Scattered throughout the unconscious lie numerous ovals with a "C" for *complexes* in the middle and a funnel tapering down to a letter "*A*" for *arche-*

type, which is at the core of a complex. We will explain these later.

Finally, at the bottom of this map are found the flames of the *primordial fire.* This image reminds us that the collective unconscious underlies the entirety of the map. It is here where primitive forces dwell and potent symbols, fears, and inspirations gradually emerge.

The External World

The external world is the easiest part of the map to understand. It represents everything we know as our world. It is everything we can touch, see, and hear and everything present in the physical world with which we interact, including people, objects, and other creatures. The external world contrasts with our internal experience. Our internal experience is harder to grasp and understand, particularly the unconscious realm of which we are not usually aware.

The Ego

The *ego* rests on the surface of the unconscious and occupies the center of consciousness. It is the "I" who speaks, and it is what *I* am aware of when *I* contemplate myself. It lies on the boundary between what we know and what we don't know. It is what we understand consciously of our experience of being human. It acts and sets projects in motion, while encompassing all the traits and characteristics by which we consciously "know ourselves." It is informed and affected by all our memories, traumas, emotions, and facts as well as everything we can consciously sense in our bodies. When we have a "flash of insight," it is often the awareness of something unconscious breaking though to our conscious *ego* awareness.

The Persona

The *persona*, the mountain range, separates our conscious *ego* from the external world and interacts with it. The eye between the *ego* and the external world emphasizes the fact that we look out to the world from our *ego*'s perspective. It is through our senses that we perceive the world around us, and this is represented by the eye looking out. What the world sees as it looks back at us is our *persona*. Thus, in this map, when friends, family, or really anyone looks at us and forms an opinion of us, they are not looking inside our *ego*, but rather at the *persona*, the mask we allow them to see. They see *persona*; they never see the "true us," only the part of ourselves that the *persona* allows them to see. Our *persona* varies, depending on what role we are in. At work, I might be a doctor. Perhaps I dress the part of a doctor by wearing a white coat or other professional clothes. I use language common to physicians, "doctor talk." I sound professional and may even find myself using big words and professional jargon that reinforces my identity and perhaps convinces me and others of my standing. My work *persona* allows me to function more freely and smoothly in my role. When I go home at night, however, if I were to forget to take off my "doctor *persona*" and not put on my "spouse *persona*," bad things will happen. I might order my spouse around, use wordy or professional jargon, insist on things being done my way, etc. At home, the aspects of my *persona* identified with my doctor *persona* are no longer adaptive; it is actually mal-adaptive. At home, I had better put on my "spouse *persona*" or my "father *persona*." With these *personas*, I am less professional; I am more likely to laugh, joke and roll around on the floor with my children. We put on a vast array of *personas* in the course of our lives, including student, friend, mentor, mentee, athlete, partygoer, rock star, social activist, etc.

The *Shadow*

Our *shadow* is the contrary image of our *persona*, its opposite. For every aspect of how we try to present ourselves to the world through our *persona*, an opposite part of our personality gets split off and stored in the *shadow*. If I have worked to make my *persona* come across as a friendly, helpful, and encouraging person, that means that the opposite of those traits, an unfriendly, unhelpful, discouraging person, becomes split off and deposited in my unconscious *shadow*. The intensity of this phenomenon appears to vary in direct proportion with how intense and one-sided my *persona* becomes. A person who presents his or her *persona* to others as an extremely righteous, pious and devoted person lacking any anger or negativity is likely creating an unconscious *shadow* with powerful, cruel, immoral, and irreverent qualities. When the *shadow* makes its presence known, it can be very energetic and forceful in the way it expresses the opposite characteristics. The news has been full of pious preachers speaking out intensely against behaviors they regard as sinful, only to find themselves scandalously caught in those very same actions. One explanation of this is that the more pious their *persona* becomes, the more energized and immoral their *shadow* becomes. Often it is only a matter of time before the unacceptable *shadow* will erupt and become exposed to the public. This sort of *reversal* can be shocking, but it can also be the beginning of a new and more authentic life if handled properly.

Typically, unless we have done a lot of personal work on ourselves, the contents of our *shadow* are hidden and unknown to us. The less we understand about our *shadow* side, the more likely we are to unknowingly act from it, often in ways that hurt others. It is crucial for us to recognize we have a *shadow* side and take steps to deal with it in healthy ways. This consists mostly of becoming conscious of aspects of *shadow* through paying attention to our dreams, to what we find objectionable in others, to what we envy, and by exploring the moments of *reversals* when the *shadow* erupts.

Anima and Animus

 Buried within our unconscious lies another figure that holds the neglected sides of our masculinity or femininity. One hundred years ago, as Carl Jung was developing these theories, gender was more rigidly defined within society. It was seldom tolerated in the Victorian Age for men to show much of their feminine side or vice versa. Thus, a man who went through life embodying mostly masculine qualities remained unaware of an undeveloped and unconscious feminine figure in his psyche that Jung called the *anima*. It is through the *anima* that a man is able to connect with his softer, more soulful, and perhaps more creative side. When he tears up, swells with intense emotions, or is more driven by the heart than the head, he is likely connecting to his *anima*.

This *anima* might come to him in dreams as a sensual or soulful woman. She is his guide to this deeper place within his personality. She is pregnant with new life, heralding the future.

Traditionally, women had the opposite development challenge to their identity. They were discouraged from pursuing demanding, male-dominated careers and rarely pursued public roles of power and authority. An unconscious masculine figure typically lived hidden away in their unconscious, a personality with strength, determination, and warrior-like power that Jung called the *animus*. In dreams, this figure often comes to women as a powerful male figure.

In the second half of a woman's life, she might distance herself from an overly nurturing role and develop a second career with a stronger, more forceful, and public personality. At such times, her *animus* is surfacing.

This paradigm has shifted dramatically over the last few decades as gender became more fluid within individuals and society in general. Men are no longer forced into solely masculine expressions of their personality, just as women are allowed more freedom of expression. Nonetheless, whatever gender elements we incline toward, the opposite gender develops unconscious power within our *anima/animus*. Connecting to those opposite gender traits allows us to become more whole and complete.

Complexes

 Scattered throughout the unconscious zone of our map are numerous *complexes*. We have symbolized them as a "C" within an oval that funnels down toward the letter "*A*." Each one of us has countless *complexes* within our unconscious.

A *complex* is a sort of subpersonality with its own set of charged emotions that cluster around certain areas or triggers in our lives, often a trauma. You have probably already heard many of the common complexes that have made their way into our vocabulary such as *mother complex, father complex, money complex, Oedipal complex, hero complex, Napoleon complex, Peter Pan complex, lover complex,* etc. Just hearing the title of the complexes likely brings to mind a fair amount of what they encompass. Thus, a person gripped by a money complex may irrationally fear poverty and financial need. Even though he has plenty of money, his fear drives him to hoard more and more. One might name it a *Scrooge complex* after the Charles Dickens character in *A Christmas Carol*. Those who struggle with a *hero complex*, on the other hand, may find themselves irrationally drawn toward rescuing others who may not even need their help. The more powerful a *complex*, the less aware we will be when we fall into it and the more our behavior is controlled by it. Our friends, family, and lovers, though, are painfully aware when we are in the grips of these *complexes,* even as we irrationally defend our behaviors.

A particular point of Jungian psychology is that at the core of every complex lies an *archetype,* in our drawings noted as the letter "*A.*" Thus, at the heart of someone's *hero complex* lies the *archetype* of the hero. This archetype is present in hero images known throughout history and embodies all the heroic traits to which humanity has ever been exposed. We can imagine the world's most powerful hero, Hercules for example, lying at the heart of this *complex.* It is that intense energy that a person in the grips of a hero complex is tapping into. These moments can be precarious for those trapped in the complex or, on the other hand, may even result in admirable deeds.

The Archetypal Self

Within the framework of Jungian psychology, the *ego* is technically a complex where we hold our conscious self-identity. Remembering that at the core of every *complex* lies an *archetype,* within the core of the *ego complex* lies the *archetypal Self.* It can be referred to by its full name, the *archetypal Self,* or simply the *Self.* By convention we capitalize the *Self* to note its elements of totality and even sacredness, similar to how *God* & *He/His/Him* are capitalized in the Christian scripture. The *Self* is humanity's (as well as each individual's) grand organizing principle. While many have referred to the *archetypal Self* as God, it may be better to think of it as godlike with infinite, boundless possibilities that we often associate with phrases like a *higher power* or a sum of all the conscious and unconscious elements within our universe. It is *the Alpha and the Omega*, the beginning and the end, the *totality* and the *singularity* combined as one. It is hard to write about the *archetypal Self* without lapsing into mysticism and using grandiose metaphors. It is truly ineffable, and words fail to capture it.

The Primordial Fire

 We added the *primordial fire* to the bottom of our map in an effort to show some of the profound archetypal forces underlying these structures. The *primordial fire* represents the initial source of psychic energy and the animating forces throughout human history and even the history of the universe. It drives survival, evolution, creativity, and such instincts as sexuality and hunger. When we are depressed, we have lost contact with the *primordial fire*. When we are manic, we may become engulfed in its flames. At times, the fire envelopes the planet, such as during the world wars or at other times of profound conflict or social upheaval. It has deep veins in the psyche, and it runs like lava beneath the crust of the earth, erupting during these intense times.

This is a collective fire that has been burning throughout the ages. Billy Joel's haunting words, "We didn't start the fire, It was always burning since the world's been turning," powerfully capture the metaphor of its ceaseless flames.

Before we dive more deeply into the ideas of *ego*, here are a few suggestions that emerge from this map.

A Few Precepts to Keep in Mind....

Don't let the world define you. Blaze your own path through!

This is particularly hard for young people. There is so much to do in those early years—excel in high school and college, find the right career, find a life partner, raise children, etc. There is nothing wrong with these things, and indeed many of them are important to pursue, but sometimes these expectations are thrust upon us against our will, and they run contrary to our true nature. Looking through the lens of our map, we must be careful that the *persona* we construct retains authenticity; we must listen to our *shadow's* ferocity; we must avoid being ensnared by our *complexes* and we must tap into the inspiration of our *anima/animus*. Only by encompassing this totality, both conscious and unconscious, can we hope to discern our unique path and follow our true self.

Listen to your nighttime dreams. Keep a dream journal.

A key principle of Jungian psychology is the crucial importance of our dreams during sleep. Dreams bubble up from the collective unconscious and are informed by the *archetypal Self*. All dreams have meaning for us, telling us something we do not yet know but need to know. Write down your nighttime dreams in a journal. Reflect on them the next day and ask yourself what the various elements of the dream remind you of. Avoid the simplicity of a "dream symbol dictionary," as you will need to do the hard work yourself and not rely on someone else's interpretations. If you can, work with a Jungian analyst or other therapist who works with dreams from that perspective. Join or start a dream group where people share and reflect on dreams in a nonjudgmental and noncritical environment. Use your dreams to develop your own personalized *Map of the Soul*.

Listen to your daytime dreams. Keep a daytime journal.

Consider keeping a daytime journal as well for any thoughts, emotions, creative impulses, or inspirations you might have. You can even write out dialogues with other parts of yourself, including *shadow* figures, *anima* figures or characters from your nighttime dreams. Notice the occasions when you undergo a reversal, and the *shadow* erupts. Ask questions and get to know these interior parts of yourself. Wonder about the present and dream about the future. Remain curious about all elements of yourself, both your interior world as well as how you interact with others. This curiosity will keep you on your path of growth.

Stay aware of your dark side (your *shadow*). Own it when it flares up and utilize its strength.

Unfortunately, ignoring our dark side is a common trap that we all fall into from time to time. We convince ourselves that we have tamed our inner darkness, only to have it reappear abruptly. When our darkness erupts, it has free rein to plunge us into various destructive paths. It is vitally important that we stay aware of our *shadow* and the hurtful prejudices, stereotypes, and superior attitudes we hold.

Stay connected to your *shadow*. Dialogue with it, listen to it, and observe how it is projected onto people and situations in your life, like a movie projected onto a screen. Acknowledge to others when your darker self has taken over and you have done things that you regret. Growth and individuation can only happen if we stay aware of our dark self and are willing to confront our less appealing qualities.

Stay connected to your body.

Avoid the trap of remaining too much in your head and disconnected from your body and the outside world. This is a trap that many Jungians and other intellectual types fall into. Looking solely at ideas, concepts, and archetypes without also looking at how they embody themselves in our physical world can prove to be a costly mistake. Listen to your body. Try to understand when it hurts, grumbles, or has a painful memory buried within it. Enjoy your body when it wants to dance, run, or play with reckless abandon.

Stay creative no matter what, and express this creativity.

Stay connected to whatever forms of creativity enliven your soul. Expressions are not only works of art like paint on a canvas, but include dance, prose, molding clay, playing music, using your voice, and countless other expressions. Creativity is a great way of tapping into the *primordial energy* in a healthy way that fuels our growth and individuation.

Know something about your personality make up, its strengths and challenges.

Stay curious about who you are and how your personality challenges and strengthens you. Seek an understanding of Carl Jung's ideas of introversion, extroversion, thinking, feeling, intuition, etc. Knowing who we are in these ways and how we engage with important people in our lives not only helps us to understand our behaviors but also helps us optimize how we engage with others.

Remember the arc of life and that young adulthood, midlife and elder years have very different callings.

It is important to consider where we are in our life's course. In our early years, we are typically building our psychic structures, our personality, our desires, our relationships, and our vocations. Hopefully, we do so with passion and a sense of calling. By midlife, we have already built these structures and we may be more occupied with a productive career, a growing family, or other challenges.

Often in midlife, there is a need for a significant course correction. We must stay alert and listen for that. By our elder years, we are on the other side of the arc of life, declining in some areas while deepening in others. We are typically exiting careers and mentoring those around us. We are often more spiritual and are nurturing our inner connection to a higher reality. While each of us needs to find our own expressions within these typical patterns, it is helpful to remember that the map serves us differently depending on the stage of our life's journey.

Remain true to yourself.

We must remain true to ourselves! But what does that really mean? Of course, it means different things to different people. We propose that it involves the vital quest of discovering what you are uniquely called to in this world. It is breaking free of the molds that others attempt to put you in as you claim your unique inheritance as a member of the human race. Regardless of how your true path unfolds, you must at all costs, listen to your gentle, whispering inner voice and honor the signs that life offers you.

Ego, Consciousness and the "I"
By Murray Stein

Consciousness is simply awareness, sentience, and has no particular center. When you're awake, you're aware, usually of something around you. Consciousness is simply awakeness. Awakeness is the ability to observe and register what's around us, to open our eyes, to be conscious of our environment. Other animals show various degrees of awakeness, or consciousness, as well. In fact, their awareness of their environments can be much sharper than ours. But a human being's consciousness is something very special in the animal world. It seems to be unique. It is able to think and say "I," and it is self-reflective.

The ego rises out of the unconscious like an island from the sea and takes its place in consciousness as its center. It is an "I"-land. A human infant, even a fresh newborn, has consciousness but not a defined ego yet. When a baby is born, the midwife will clean her eyes and wrap her in a blanket. She opens her eyes and looks around. We're pretty sure she doesn't know what she's looking at. The whole world is still unfamiliar. But she is definitely awake and taking in visual and auditory perceptions. When the eyes are open and they're looking around, we imagine that there is a conscious being there. She's alive, and the eyes are taking in something, but consciousness doesn't depend on eyes alone. The ears, skin, and other senses awaken and are a part of consciousness as well. We know that there is even a kind of consciousness in the womb before the eyes have seen anything definite. That little infant had been conscious for a time already in its uterine life, registering sounds and reacting to various stimuli. A kind of preliminary consciousness awakens already in the womb. Nobody knows exactly when it starts being a part of the infant's experience. The creation of consciousness is a spark of light in the dark waters of the womb. The birth of the ego comes later.

The absence of consciousness in a body means either a state of deep sleep or coma, or death. An unawake body is not necessarily a corpse, but it may be. When you see a body laid out in the funeral parlor and you go up close and it's a person you've known, you're aware that there's something essential missing. What is it? Traditionally, people have thought that the soul has left the body behind and gone elsewhere. The absence of consciousness, even if it's a body asleep, gives us the feeling that the soul if absent. The dead person is not just sleeping, however, and there is no longer the possibility of consciousness returning and animating the body. The corpse is the same material but without energy, unenlivened matter. There, consciousness is no longer a possibility.

Consciousness is what the ego knows, and the unconscious is what it doesn't know. One can also be vaguely conscious of something on the fringe of consciousness; in other words, the ego can know it a little bit, but not all the way down to its roots. One of the purposes of analysis is to extend the range of the ego so it knows more of what's going on in the psyche as a whole and thus is able to extend the range of consciousness. What's outside of consciousness is the unconscious. This includes most of the world, inner and outer. Everything you don't know is unconscious to you. If you don't know how many moons revolve around Saturn, that is in the unconscious for you. That's as unconscious as the archetypes of the collective unconscious are to you. Unconsciousness is simply a term that refers to whatever you don't know. Whatever is not a content of your consciousness belongs to the unconscious. Of course, we make a distinction between the psychic unconscious and the material unconscious. Science attempts to bring both into greater consciousness.

Consciousness accompanies the aliveness of matter. It gives living matter the ability to interact, react, and engage with the surrounding environment.

When the living body is asleep, it is still somewhat conscious in the sense that it can react to environmental stimuli like noise, heat, cold, etc., and when one is dreaming, consciousness is active and interacting with figures and environments in the inner world of the psyche. The dream is experience every bit as vivid and convincing as experience while we are awake. A dream feels as real as any other experiences we might have. We're usually the same person in our dreams as we are in waking life, but occasionally we're not.

We can make a distinction between consciousness per se and the contents of consciousness. The contents are what you're *conscious of* when you're conscious. These contents of consciousness can be sorted into two kinds: inner and outer. When you're conscious of inner contents, you're aware of your emotions, your thoughts, your feelings, fantasies, images, memories, etc. These belong to your "inner world." If somebody asks you, "What are you thinking about?" and you tell them about feelings, you are talking about something that can't be observed or confirmed by anybody else. An outer content of consciousness refers to objects that are readily observed by others. You are conscious of the world around you. If somebody says, "What are you thinking about?" and you say: "Well, I'm looking at the trees, the plants, the people around and enjoying the beauty of it all." That's what is occupying your consciousness at that moment. In a sense, all contents of consciousness are inner, but the reference is different.

There is another important distinction to be made, and that is between consciousness as such and a center of consciousness. Carl Jung defined the ego as the center of consciousness. If the ego is the center of consciousness, however, this doesn't mean it's necessarily active. It can be passive. If the ego is not active and you're simply observing something whether inner or outer, the ego is present but as an observer. You're just looking at a person or scene or observing a thought or feeling without reacting. The ego is there but only as a witness. It is not doing or willing or acting; it is just "seeing." Often we think of the ego as active and therefore often as interfering or distorting, but this needn't be the case.

For some religions and schools of meditation, an important spiritual objective is to have consciousness but no active center of willing or thinking or desiring. The goal is to achieve pure consciousness without any ego participation or interference. This means ego detachment. You just observe things. You don't try to control them. You don't try to do anything with them, you just observe them and pass on. Very few of us can do this for long. The ego tends to become active, to want change, or to do something, or to prefer one thing over another. The ego tends to become engaged with what we're observing. You get emotionally involved in what you are witnessing, and you start wishing and desiring and hoping and planning and doing. Your ego becomes activated and participates in the story, even if only vicariously through identification with the objects being brought into consciousness. You can see the rudimentary states of this activation in infancy. Obviously, the infant doesn't have a commanding knowledge of her environment or interest in controlling it, but she's noticing things. She notices shapes and colors and movement, and pretty soon it's evident that certain objects are familiar to her and some are very pleasurable and she reaches out for them and wants them. Others she fends off and doesn't want. There is an early center of consciousness, the first signs of an ego becoming active and willing.

The "I"

When we speak about "ego," we're speaking about "I," your "I-ness." Whenever you say, "I," you're making reference to your ego: "I want; I'm going; I plan; I think; I feel." You're speaking from and about your ego and saying "who" is speaking. It's the center of your consciousness at the moment and it expresses your identity. If you stop for a moment, close your eyes, and reflect on this "I," you will get a special feeling about yourself, maybe even mysterious. It feels like something that's been there for your entire life, but what is it, this "I"?

Does this "I" ever really change from the time you cry for your mother when you're 2 or 3 years old to when you cry about losing your parents when they have grown old and you are middle aged? Many things change, for instance your body, but it is a real question to what extent the "I" develops and changes. It can certainly grow stronger or weaker, but does the essence change?

The ego-centered consciousness of human beings seems different from other animals' consciousness because of our verbal abilities. We can speak with and about our "I" while other animals do not, at least as far as we can discern. They seem to have something like an ego, a center of consciousness. The individual cat or dog is very focused when it is after its prey. And animals want to control their environments to a certain extent by marking their territory and so forth. They respond to their names. Perhaps there is no essential difference between the human ego and the ego of other animal species. It is just that we have language to speak about it, and with language we can reflect and deepen our understanding. Is the cat gazing into the far distance quietly reflecting on itself? We don't know.

At a certain point, our names and our "I" become fused. If somebody asks you who you are, you give them your name. If your name is called out, you respond instantly and spontaneously. It is as though your "I" and your name were one. Your name is something you identify with before you can even say "I." But people change their names. Women in patriarchal societies have done this for countless generations. They change their last names; sometimes they change their first names. If you join a religious order, you might change your name. You might become Mother Teresa, and Teresa wasn't your name before that. Names can come and go, and all that surrounds the "I" can change. You could have been given another name, and the response would be the same. People change their names, and yet their ego remains the same as before: You have the same "I" under a different name. Everything that gets put onto or into the "I" is secondary to it. All that your ego identifies with, all that you claim as your own and feel very strongly about, can change. But the "I" itself doesn't change very much, if at all. Perhaps we could even say that "I" is the soul. After you die, your name remains famous, as Julius Caesar's did, but the ego is no longer present.

The Wandering Ego

While I was driving one day, I suddenly realized I was on a route that I hadn't intended to take. I was thinking about other things. I drove within the speed limits because I now have made a habit of doing that after receiving a couple of tickets for speeding. And I must have noticed the other cars on the road because I didn't run into any of them. Obviously, I was conscious. I wasn't asleep, but my ego wasn't quite fully present to driving. That's why I took a route that I had not intended. It was the old path I had driven many times before, and the new path required more of my ego's attention. I was elsewhere. My ego was occupied with other things. I was thinking about what I was going to do that day, about when I needed to finish some project or other, about difficult conversations I'd had over the prior weekend, etc.

What I'm getting at is that there is a difference between consciousness as such and the ego. Consciousness can be spread out across several screens of activity taking place at the same time. It can be running on automatic pilot in one area (in this case, driving the car) while the ego is busily occupied elsewhere. We are able to divide our attention in this way. I had to get into the car, put the key in the ignition, turn on the engine and set off in a certain direction. The ego was partially involved in that. But then the ego was engaged elsewhere, and a kind of robotic consciousness took over the task of driving that well-learned route. If something had suddenly come up that required focal attention, the ego would have returned and taken note of it. If another car had swerved sharply in front of me—"oh my goodness, what's going on?"—the ego would be right back and ready to react. But in the meantime, who's driving the car? It isn't the ego. It is consciousness based on certain habits and conditioning.

In many areas and for many tasks, consciousness is largely trained and conditioned and doesn't require the ego's control or direction. So, the ego can leave it to its own devices. The ego is where the "I" is in the field of consciousness. The "I" can move around in this field and enter into other frames of consciousness while the former frame runs on of its own accord out of training and habit. The "I" may attend to driving the car, or it may wander off and be occupied with something else like plans for the day or evening ahead. The "I" can dip into the stream of consciousness at any point. It has the freedom to be present to the moment, or to go daydreaming about the distant future, or to indulge in remembering the past. It has freedom of movement in time and space, while the body is fixed. We sometimes call this disassociation. The ego becomes disassociated with what is going on in one frame of consciousness and is somewhere else. This may be a defense against pain, or it may be quite a normal situation with no emotional threat involved.

This wandering ego occurs in countless situations. When I'm lecturing, people in the audience will naturally drift in and out. One moment a person is listening to me, and then I say something that triggers some associations, and the ego drifts off into those thoughts and memories. Eventually (hopefully), the person's center of attention will return, and the ego will come back to the lecture. We do the same thing when we're listening to someone in a conversation. Our associations draw us away in a certain direction, and then we come back. We might apologize and ask: "What did you say? I missed something."

Our egos tend to wander. It's a rare and well-disciplined ego that will stay in one place for any length of time.

The Ego
By Murray Stein

When we think about the ego, or we are in the ego, it seems as if it's the center of the world. It seems as if it's the most important part of the psyche because it's the position or seat that we occupy. Moreover, we delineate the world by our ego; that is, we put ourselves in the center of the world. So, if we were to make a map of the psyche, based on the ego's position and perception, we'd put the ego right in the middle, the most important figure of the entire map.

But we know that the ego is actually something of a pimple on the body of the psyche. It's much smaller than the psyche as a whole. If you think of the entirety of the unconscious, it is immensely larger than the ego. So when you want to map the psyche, the ego has to be put in perspective. We could compare the ego to the sun. Planets revolve around it. The sun is the center of our solar system, but the sun itself is a part of a galaxy of millions of stars. And so, if you look at the sun in the perspective of the whole galaxy, you see that it is small and, indeed, almost insignificant when taken as a part of a whole. So that's a way of thinking about the ego. It is important but it also takes itself too seriously.

Ego versus Persona

The persona is the mask that the ego puts on itself in order to adapt to the world. In a sense, the persona is a function of the ego, and it serves the ego's purposes to adapt itself to the social and cultural situation. But in the end, ego and persona are closely related. It is possible for the ego to identify so thoroughly with the persona that the ego doesn't realize there's even a difference between itself and the persona. In fact, most people are not aware of their persona because it's so closely glued to the ego that it's the primary perception of who one is. You dress yourself up and take care of your appearance so as to be presentable to the group or the culture of which you want to be a part. The ego is a part of that and is in the world. The ego is interested in the world, and it needs to adapt to the world. The ego and the persona differ, but these differences are more functional than structural. For instance, suppose you are the head of a clinic, or you are a doctor or a teacher; then, in those roles you assume a particular persona that's fitting to that position. When you arrive home and you are with your family, you are no longer in that role, but that is not to say you're a different person. From time to time, you might catch a glimpse of the difference by noticing how you are with the people in your professional life and how you are with the people at home. That would give you a clue as to what persona you're wearing in those situations. Each of those situations would still be encompassed by ego. The ego is functioning, and it is using the persona to adapt to situations. Now, at home, you're also in a persona of sorts. If you're a father of children: You're playing that role. It is a role you've identified with, and you take it seriously, you feel it's a really important part of your life. But still, you do play a role for the child. You're an authority figure. You have to set boundaries. Sometimes you have to structure the physical and emotional. So, you have to take responsibility for that, and when you do that, you're doing it as a "father figure." That is a persona.

Looking Inward

As the ego comes to know the unconscious, the result is not necessarily a pleasurable sense of well-being, but rather a more conscious sense of self. Because of our sensory apparatus, we're looking out at the world around us most of the time and dealing with it and adapting to it and functioning in it. When the ego turns inward instead of facing outward and looks at the unconscious, it comes upon features of personality that might be contradictory to the persona or to its sense of self.

In Jungian psychology, we talk about confronting the Shadow or becoming conscious of the Shadow. This is usually an uncomfortable realization or experience because the Shadow is made up of those parts of ourselves that we would like to look away from, perhaps even hide from ourselves or other people to avoid shame or embarrassment. When you descend into the basement of the psyche, so to speak, into the unconscious, you come across these features.

Freud did his self-analysis in the 1890s after his father died. He engaged in enough analysis of his own dreams, and out of that experience he wrote *The Interpretation of Dreams*, probably Freud's best book. What he discovered when he looked at his dreams in free association with them were features of himself that he found quite distasteful. He recognized that he was competitive, he was envious, that he felt guilty about his misdeeds in certain cases. In other words, he was becoming conscious of himself.

This awareness of those parts of ourselves that we usually hide from, repress, or suppress are one of the first things we discover when we start looking at the unconscious. When you go deeper into the unconscious, you might discover your animal nature as an extension of the Shadow to some extent. This, too, is a part of your physical nature. People dream about animals a lot, and if you look at the animals and what they symbolize, we can see features of the personality that might be uncomfortable or distasteful to the person, but they give us important information about our nature.

It's much better to be aware of this than to be unconscious of it because if you're aware of it, you have a chance to offset its effects a bit, to protect other people from the effects of your Shadow or your animal behavioral instincts.

It's a little bit like becoming conscious of coronavirus in your environment. It's not a pleasant thing to think about, but it's better to be aware that it's out there than to be unaware. If you are aware, then you can protect yourself from it and protect other people. If you discover you've been infected with the virus, you wear a mask so you don't spread it to other people.

Looking Upward

But there are also parts of the psyche that are much more pleasant to contemplate, including various Archetypal images, spiritual aspects of our unconscious selves. As we fill out the knowledge of the self as we experience it in our dreams, imagination, and so on, we realize there is a balance between the positive and the negative. Jung spoke about the self as a union of the opposites. It's made up of opposite features, qualities, tendencies, and these balance each other out so that you get a mandala-like picture, a round, 360-degree picture of the self, insofar as you're able. And the various features balance themselves out against their opposites, in that circle or mandala.

The ego also has an impulse that draws it toward more noble or inspiring or expansive aspects. We define the ego as the center of consciousness, but it's more than that. It's also a container that has active features. One of those active features is curiosity and an interest to learn and to expand the consciousness that surrounds it. So, unless the ego is heavily defended against painful topics or not wanting to look into the darkness of the unconscious or explore the world, as long as the defenses don't get in the way, the ego is interested to know more. It's like an epistemological instinct. We want to know.

That certainly was strong in Jung's makeup, perhaps his strongest instinct: He wanted *to know*, to understand. He was very curious about himself and the world around him.

Ego's Resistance and Stages of Transformation

The ego resists change and experiences transformation as a sort of death. Transformation is a kind of death and rebirth process, so demise isn't the correct word. It's a fear of dying. An analyst, David Rosen, who wrote on suicide, called it *egocide*.

We undergo the experience of transformation several times in our lives. There are big periods of transformation and there are much smaller ones, but a big one is transformation from childhood to adulthood, and that period is called adolescence. During adolescence, we're going through a transformation from being a child to being an adult, but there's a lot going on physically, physiologically, and psychologically in our being. An adolescent takes a new form, develops a new sense of identity, and begins to function in the world in quite a different way.

Another period of transformation is midlife, when we move from the first half of life into the second half of life, classically around the ages between the late 30s and the late 40s. Then there's another one at the end of life in old age. This is when one retires or begins to withdraw from one's activities and develop other interests, maybe spiritual interests or reflections that are not so much engaged in an active way in the world.

But each of these transitions is a transformation process that includes a death and rebirth, a death to what has been and a birth to new possibilities, and that includes a new sense of identity. So you could think of metaphors like the caterpillar turning into a butterfly. There's an in-between stage in the cocoon, where the caterpillar melts down and dies to what it was, and a new form appears with wings, and then it comes out of the shell as a butterfly. This is also like a snake shedding its skin, and when it outgrows that skin, once again it sheds. Having grown a new skin, it goes on in its life.

These periods of transformation typically include death anxiety. Adolescents have a lot of it. It sets in yet again at midlife. People typically experience death around them. Death anxiety is very much a part of that midlife crisis. And again, at old age when death is becoming more and more of a present reality. Resistance to change can be strong, and the psyche often forces change upon a person; people seldom go into it voluntarily. You see that especially going into old age with people going to great lengths and spending a lot of energy and money to maintain an identity that probably is no longer really appropriate for them in their stage of life. With each transformation we become a new kind of person with a new or different identity. If people can relax and accept that change may not be necessarily bad, if they can go with the flow and move through it in a graceful way, they may realize these transformations as simply a part of life.

Basic Trust and the Early Years

What helps to organize and solidify the container of the ego consciousness? The most important thing in the earliest years of childhood is a reliable environment; that is, a reliable physical, emotional, and interpersonal environment. The young person is basically helpless in the world at first and instinctively relies on caregivers to provide the necessary containment, nurturance, protections, protective surroundings. If that's not there, a serious compromise in ego development can take place. Anxieties can haunt a person for the rest of their lives because their initial environment was not reliable or was not suitable, was not tuned into the needs that they had as an infant.

What contributes to the formation of a strong ego in the long run is a consistent and reliable environment in the early years. It doesn't have to be perfect, but it has to be *good enough*, as Donald Winnicott said, to allow the ego to feel some confidence in the basis of life that the child will be held and cared for. And if that base confidence, that basic trust, as Erik Erikson described it is not there, the kinds of anxieties that emerge can have profound effects.

The lack of basic trust can remain a part of the ego and really hinder the ego from developing a sense of confidence in itself and in life during the later years.

Early Trauma

Upon the basic structure of the early years, other aspects of the personality form like accretions. If the early years are filled with trauma and neglect, these early scars may remain evident in the later years. However, the psyche has tremendous resources for self-healing. This has been demonstrated in therapy with children. For example, consider the work of Eva Pattis Zoja with children from very troubled or war-torn areas of the world who had suffered severe trauma or who had suffered as migrants or who were abandoned in orphanages. She discovered that sandplay sessions over a period of 10 weeks with an adult observer had tremendous reconstructive effects on the child's attitude toward himself or herself, toward others, and that the child's behavior in school showed improvement. She mentions the immense resources for healing the psyche has within itself if the opportunity is provided for it to emerge and to heal itself.

A lot depends on what happens after people are traumatized. Are they in a situation where they can have guided therapy that will allow them to work that through and let the psyche use its resources for healing? Or does the trauma become embedded in the psyche in such a way that it continues to interfere with the good, normal ego development in the future. I don't underestimate how much the psyche can heal itself, but it needs an opportunity to do that, and that's why we're around as therapists.

The environment the ego relies upon for its proper development should be attuned to the needs of the infant. What happens is if it's not well attuned, or if it's totally unattuned, is that the infant can survive physically and grow and look more or less intact and functional, but there is such an underlying anxiety about safety and security that it develops excessively active and strong defenses against any possible dangers that the child may face. A strong ego is not fragile; it can face dangers, get bounced around, suffer failures and losses, and still it recovers. But a fragile ego cannot take very much before it breaks. If there isn't a good beginning with a solid, stable, reliable environment, this kind of fragility develops. To protect themselves, these people then build up enormous defenses so that if they ever come close to being wounded or attacked, or engage in situations where there is some possibility of suffering, they practically become like wild animals. It's what we observe with borderline personality disorder: huge amounts of rage and anger, attacking others before they themselves can come under attack. It is a sort of paranoid, schizoid defense because of this feeling that they are in danger, so they exaggerate the danger. That exaggeration comes from their early experience.

I'm thinking of a person I worked with for a number of years who was put into an orphanage when she was born and brought back home by her parents when she was about 6 to 9 months old. She never did attach well to her parents after that. The orphanage provided only the most basic care, it wasn't regulated, and there wasn't really enough food for the children, so it was a struggle to get through life. This woman is strong physically, but she has this hair-trigger sensitivity to being insulted or attacked or demeaned, so that she will size you up immediately, and either you're a friend or a foe. You're either on her side or you're on the enemy's side. That all stems from this early sense of insecurity that was built into her system, and the defenses are there to protect her. She's a lovely person if she's not threatened. But if she is, she becomes very violent.

Exposure to severe, repeated trauma, and maybe even intentional cruelty can have a very lasting impact, and often this depends on the age and the kind of abuse. One of the problems that can develop is an enormous sense of guilt and low self-esteem because people feel responsible for the bad things that happened to them. They come to believe that they were bad and that it was their fault that a parent abused them (whether physically, sexually, verbally, or emotionally). They take in those messages of "You're bad," "It's your fault," or "If you say anything, you'll be punished," so the trauma becomes a secret, and the guilt builds. In order to offset that, they might develop defense mechanisms that tell them that they're OK. For instance, they look for affirmation from other people. This is the problem with those with narcissistic personality disorder. They can't affirm themselves, so they have to get it from the outside. They don't have the inner resources to say, "I'm OK. I'm fine. I've done a few things bad or wrong, but I can forgive myself and work it through." Instead of that, they have to get the affirmation from outside, so they perform to get the gleam in the eye of the others and to get affirmation from other people around them. It becomes a mirror in them. Everyone is a mirror for them—do they like me, admire me—but deep underneath this, there is a deep anxiety. If the acclamation from others is interrupted, you can get a collapse perhaps into depression. They struggle with deep questions about their self-worth, whether they're guilty of misdeeds, or bringing terrible things on themselves. They exaggerate their own responsibility.

Childhood Trauma in Adults

Despite deep, basic anxiety that people might have endured in childhood, they may come into their adult years and appear quite well on the surface apart from the evidence of their exaggerated defenses. Indeed, they can be extremely functional, intelligent, educated, hold down good jobs. But generally, they can't sustain long-term relationships very well. When they encounter a crisis, the other becomes the enemy too quickly and to an extreme degree. There's a rupture of the relationship as they cannot bear to be too close to potential enemies. Relationships become very difficult to maintain over a long period. Such people might not be so successful in types of jobs where you have to be a team player and work well with other people. As long as they can work by themselves, they may do well. Sometimes they're very creative and may find it best to work on their own and not bother too much with other people around them.

There are adults who endure fragile states that require ceaseless affirmation. If the flow of other people's acclaim is interrupted, even for brief periods, they can collapse into horrible depression. They may seek out ways to make themselves feel better through drugs or alcohol or other means of killing off the terrible feelings of low self-esteem, self-hate and self-accusation. If you're not being assured by a partner who's mirroring you, or the network of people who are in a work situation, I think the vulnerability to that kind of collapse is quite severe. They may lash out ferociously, and there is, of course, such a thing as narcissistic rage. If the mirroring isn't adequate or the mirroring from another person reveals a flaw or a fault, then the defenses can come into action that would appear in the form of an attack of rage designed to try to overcome the person (or enemy) who is pointing out their inadequacies. The problem is that when this person is confronted with an inadequacy, it confirms what they already know to be inadequacies. It's as if they're fighting against themselves, fighting against your own knowledge about yourself. It's a battle within and a battle without.

Substance Use Disorders (Addiction)

For some unfortunate people, substance use becomes a sort of balm for the troubled soul. However, the ego becomes enslaved in the throes of addiction. How do you understand that descent?

When it becomes addiction, there is a metaphysical component to it, as if the body is craving for the substance and more. The ego is more or less helpless. The intensity of the addiction is greater than the amount of energy the ego has at its disposal to exert its will. Even people who want sobriety and want to stop using drugs often simply can't do it, that's why we have treatment centers to help them. It might be a terrible struggle to get rid of the physical addiction until the ego is able to make a free decision, but the descent into the addiction means the substance is working, that is, it is killing the pain, whether it's psychic pain or physical pain.

But it has another effect beyond helping the ego cope with pain because it introduces chemical dependency. Of course, there are also psychological addictions, where it's more of the ego question, and a strong ego can face the psychological part of the addiction. However, a weak ego is deeply helpless in the face of psychological addictions. It's usually a combination of a psychological and a physical addiction that puts people into clinics and treatment centers.

Higher Power and the Archetype

The first step of the 12-step program of Alcoholics Anonymous, a program that some people have associated with an encounter with Jung, involves admitting powerlessness. Oddly, the ego that is incapable of overcoming addiction is freed by acknowledging powerlessness. Just the first step of 12 steps, but it doesn't come from Jung.

There was a patient, Bill W., who came to see Jung after having relapsed into alcoholism. Jung realized that he couldn't cure this man. Psychotherapy, the kind he had to offer, was not going to do the job. So he said to him, "I can't help you. You have to look for a higher source of help." This man eventually began to meet with another person, and they developed the 12 steps, some of which were based on principles espoused by a Christian group, the Oxford Group. The first step was to say, "I'm helpless," and that was an echo of what Jung said: "I'm helpless. I can't help you." When Bill W. heard that, he turned to his inward self, saying, "I'm helpless. I can't help myself. I have to look for a higher power to help me," and that was the beginning of his developing the 12 steps and finding that higher power.

At the risk of stretching the apocryphal story too far, one may wonder if the ego, in its efforts to awaken, might not struggle with the same sort of drama. And in this case, the higher power could be akin to the Self.

I think what Jung was suggesting was that he as another human being couldn't help Bill W. Rather, Bill W. had to find a source within himself. And Bill

W. turned to the spiritual traditions that were available to him, biblical traditions. Prayer is part of it. You don't have to pray to a specific god image, but you have to look for a source beyond the ego itself. The ego's power is limited. Most of us think we have much more power than we actually have, but all you have to do is get sick or addicted or have something catastrophic happen to realize the limitations of the power that the ego has over its own house. What we realize is that instincts are powerful as well as the complexes and the Archetypes. These are mighty powers that can overtake us, possess us, and we're relatively helpless in their grips.

Keep in mind that sometimes it's OK to be possessed by the Archetypal powers. It gives us a sense of mission. It takes us somewhere that we need to go, gives a sense of location, perhaps, and a direction. Later, we become conscious of the power that we've been given through loan by the Archetypal sources of the psyche.

The ego itself is more like a mirror. It's a spark of consciousness. Jung sometimes compared it to a light in the darkness. You have a lantern, you're in a forest. It's nighttime, and you can only see so much around you. The forest is vast, and there are animals in the forest and ghosts and goblins and who knows what out there. And you've got your little light. That's the ego in the psyche.

Jung and Freud

Freud had a three-part structure to the psyche. The ego, the conscious will, which is similar to Jung. The id, that was for Freud the main domain of the instinctive unconscious. Finally, there's the superego, and that is the internalized sense of threat from father or the authorities that if we do something wrong, we will be punished. The superego kind of keeps us on track, culturally speaking. It's part of an anxiety system that's built into the psyche to be afraid of being punished, either by oneself with the feeling of guilt or by outer authorities if we're caught.

That was Freud's setup, and then the ego has to maintain or manage this conflict between what the id wants, (the instinctual desires) and what the superego wants (obedience to the rules, the morality of the culture and proper behavior).

Jung didn't set it up like that. Jung simply said the ego is the center of consciousness. It's subject to psychic forces and outside forces, including cultural forces that must be taken into account. Is there conflict? Yes, but it's more like a spot of consciousness or like a magnet that holds the contents of consciousness together.

Now, when we say "I," what is that? Jung says in one place in his late work the ego is a more or less stable configuration of several Archetypal components. Jung also says that the ego is the center of consciousness and that it is the mirror of the Self that is the center of the total psyche, and that the ego and the Self have an inherent mirroring connection. Erich Neumann spoke of the ego-Self axis. The connection between the ego and the Self, if it's stable, gives one a sense of inner security, reliability and stability. But the ego is very dependent on other people and other parts of the psyche supporting it, including the Self and other Archetypal energies.

Dream-ego and Waking-ego

In most dreams the "I," or what we call the dream-ego, is very similar to your sense of self when you're awake. When you recount the dream, you say, "I was walking down the road and I saw a lion coming out of the woods and I ran for cover." The "I" in the dream is very similar to the way you experience life in the waking state. So dream-ego and the waking-ego are not different in that case. But in some dreams, they're quite different.

I've seen some dreams of clients who dream that they are animals. One woman dreamed that she was a lion in St. Mark's Plaza in Venice, walking through the plaza. Another woman, I remember, dreamed that she was a butterfly. Sometimes you dream that you're another person or a different gender. Those are infrequent, but they do happen.

What we say about the dream is that it compensates for the waking state. Compensation means that it gives you something that you've left out or is lacking or you need in your ego consciousness in order to live closer to your full potential, your wholeness, or an improved state of consciousness. The dreams compensate by balancing that one-sidedness of consciousness.

If the dream-ego is very different, you would want to look at that difference. What is the dream-ego doing that waking conscious or the waking-ego, is not doing or cannot do? So in the case of the lion, it's giving a feeling of royalty and power to this person. You can say that in a waking state, the person maybe felt a lack of that kind of power. This is the power of the self; the lion is self-representation.

Now with the butterfly, that woman was too concrete, and the butterfly is anything but concrete. It's evanescent, it's ephemeral, it's the soul itself. She needed more lightness, a sense of self that had more symbolic value in her life. So, we looked at the difference and tried to interpret the ways in which the dream-ego was a compensation.

There was a German Jungian psychoanalyst, Hans Dieckmann, who wrote an essay on dream-ego in which he claimed that the dream-ego is more individuated than the waking-ego. That means that the dreaming ego can do things that the waking-ego couldn't do, or the dream-ego knows things that the waking-ego doesn't know and yet needs to know. He suggested the dream-ego is more advanced in consciousness and abilities than the waking-ego. I always try to keep that in the back of my mind when I think about this question: Is the dream-ego ahead of the waking-ego? Is it more developed; is it more individuated? It may even presage, sometimes, what the waking-ego is inclining toward.

Powerful Forces and Ego

The ego is afloat, adrift on an ocean of other forces that support and surround it. And sometimes, the winds are blowing in its favor, and sometimes, winds are blowing against it. If you read the great epics like *The Odyssey* or *The Aeneid*, you get this image of these sailors in boats, and if the gods are with them, everything is going fine, and then some god comes along and lets his anger out. Suddenly, there are high waves and hurricane-force winds, and a person is blown off course.

But that's a good picture of the ego, actually. It's in the midst of powerful forces that it can't control, but its strength is that it is awake. A resilient ego can survive a whole lot of difficulty and catastrophe going on around it. You see that in the heroes. Aeneas, in *The Aeneid* is one, as well as Odysseus in *The Odyssey*. These are wonderful stories, showing how the ego copes with difficult environments as well as the gods and all the forces for and against it. These great stories serve to give us comfort during our own storms.

Collective Ego and BTS

There is a collective level at which ego comes into play. Every tightly knit group has a kind of collective ego that the individuals participate in. It doesn't mean the individuals don't have their own egos, especially when they're not in the group. They have their own separate individual egos, but they can also be very influenced by the group unconscious and the group orientation.

So, for instance, we have mob psychology, in which something about the individuals is taken up into an emotional state where their individual egos become melted together, so to speak, into a mob. Members of the mob participate in some extreme active thing that, left to their own devices, they would not engage in. Warfare is a bit like that, too. The army tries to instill its collective ego intention, led by the general to direct the troops what to do and how to behave. And the troops will follow that and carry out their orders and do things that, under normal circumstances, they would never consider, such as killing innocent people or people who are identified as enemies.

For example, BTS, the enormously popular group of seven singers, has become a sort of collective ego. Now BTS is not the kind of a group that engages in terrible things, but the members are very tightly knit. They practice together, they live together, they perform together, they travel together. So, I think there's a very closely and very carefully developed sense of that group identity that they all participate in. When one thinks, it's as though they all think. The songs are sung by one or another, but they represent the whole group.

That group identity influences them in their individual identities so even when they're apart, they still feel that they're part of the group. "I'm a BTS member," and that probably will never leave them because it's such an intense experience over a period of 10 years. During these formative years of adolescence and early adulthood, they form these intense bonds and a common purpose that will stay with them for the rest of their lives. Even when they go their separate ways. At some point, I'm sure they will. The group will break up, and the members will have their own separate, individual lives in a much fuller way than they have had until now.

Unus Mundus

The ego that is capable of becoming immersed during war or in the midst of a mob is also capable of being swept into mysteries like those that were practiced in antiquity. People seek out the experience of merger or ecstasy. This desire to merge into something larger, grander is fundamental. When you're really by yourself and alone, it can certainly be a very nice experience. Some people love to be alone. But in those moments, you also realize how small you are in relation to the bigger scheme of things. And when you merge with another, you lose that sense of separateness. You enter into an experience of oneness with all that is.

Freud wrote about this. He said that when people fall in love, the ego loses its boundaries, and they become one. It's an experience of oneness and unity that is marvelous. Most people, when they are in love, feel at one with the world and everything that is. It's like that experience of union.

We speak about the *unus mundus* and the *anima mundi*. The experience of union with another individual or group gives you the experience of unity with the world. Some may think of that as a repeat of an experience of the reality you had when you were in your mother's womb. In the womb, there were no divisions or separation. All was one. Others may think of it as a very advanced stage of knowing that at a certain level, everything is one. It's all energy, we're all united, we're all a part of everything; this is a kind of advanced mystical state.

Ultimately, we all long for that and search for it. We find it and experience it in love, or in religious experiences, or sometimes in a dream that is like a vision of unity of all that is. Love is the glue that holds things together. Hate is the force that separates. So they're at war with each other, love and hate. They're both necessary, but that experience of oneness is something everybody longs for.

Final Thoughts on Ego
By Leonard Cruz and Steven Buser

From the moment an infant distinguishes self from nonself (or other), the ego starts to form. The earliest caregivers serve as a bridge between the child's experience of self originating within him and those that originate in the external world of reality (Winnicott, 1965). Ego is the "I" when you say, "I am" or "I want." A name lends identity to the "I." Ego identity extends in many directions, to include nationality, gender, tribe, religion, etc.

It has become fashionable to allude to ego as an impediment to deep understanding or enlightening experiences. However, the ego is necessary for the evolution of consciousness. Though Jung gave great importance to the Self, he made clear in *Aion* that the concept of the Self does not replace the ego. For Jung, the Self is the whole personality. The ego "rests on two different bases: somatic and psychic."[1] The ego is not identical with the field of consciousness upon which it rests. However, it does provide a "point of reference" for the field of consciousness.

Since it is the point of reference for the field of consciousness, the ego is the subject of all successful attempts at adaptation so far as these are achieved by the will. The ego therefore has a significant part to play in the psychic economy. Its position there is so important that there are good grounds for the prejudice that the ego is the centre of the personality, and that the field of consciousness is the psyche per se.[2]

Were it not for the distortions introduced by the ego, there might be less need to explore the unconscious realms. Jung pointed out, "It is often tragic to see how blatantly a man bungles his own life and the lives of others yet remains totally incapable of seeing how much the whole tragedy originates in himself, and how he continually feeds it and keeps it going."[3]

During the past century, the concept of an unconscious became widely understood; what the ego does not tolerate or what it finds unacceptable is repressed into unconscious realms. At the conscious level, the ego is responsible for recognizing our own image, our name, and it equips us to exercise our will and consciously make decisions and take actions.

While a strong ego benefits a person who chooses to embark on a journey of self-discovery, a *too strong* ego can be an insurmountable obstacle. A fine line exists between an ego strong enough to withstand the buffeting that life inevitably delivers and an ego so ensnared in its subjectivity that it is incapable of seeing the deeper and farther reaches of human potential. Having some understanding of the masks we wear (persona), our repressed, unacceptable psychological features (shadow), and the conscious, organizing principle (ego) gives useful tools for exploring our inner landscape.

For ego to form and develop in a healthy fashion, there must be what Dr. Stein refers to as a *reliable environment*. When this is present, ego displays remarkable continuity over the lifetime. There is a deep truth in William Wordsworth's line of verse, "The child is the father of the man." While the experience of "I" remains stable from the beginning to the end of life, its surroundings change over time. Along the way one's sense of self changes as one develops psychologically. We live into the awareness that our sense of self is continuous and ever-changing. As one becomes aware of persona, shadow, anima, animus, cultural complexes and identifications, the sense of self expands and contracts. Through this all, there is an innate wholeness that remains intact and, like the center of a mandala, brings order to the disparate features.

While Jung proposed that the ego has some amount of free or "surplus" energy at its disposal for the free will and to build culture, most people deceive themselves in thinking they have more free will than they actually possess. To a much greater extent than most people realize, they are moved by unconscious forces.

Insights and discoveries from such disparate fields as quantum physics, neuroscience, linguistics, cognitive psychology, and depth psychology have forced modern man to accept that we are mistaken to think that we are entirely the captains of our own ship. This series, *The Map of the Soul*, seeks to simply and systematically present various aspects of the psyche's structure as elucidated by C.G. Jung. This volume that is devoted to the ego readily embraces many paradoxes regarding the ego's central role in psychic life. Looked at from the subjective perspective, *das ich*, the "I" to which Freud referred, is the axis upon which personality pivots. But the ego is subject to many forces, some personal, deriving from the environment in which a person arises and others collective, deriving from a vast, unseen realm of cultural, mythic, and archetypal influence.

One of the most intriguing dimensions of the human experience emerges when people turn an examining eye (or "I") back upon themselves. Meditation, psychotherapy, philosophy, and depth psychology rely on this inherent capacity for self-examination. Nothing requires a person to undertake self-exploration, yet the nearly universal impulse to examine, understand, and evolve suggests something deep, something mysterious, something holy is taking place in us. Perhaps, we are engaged in a mysterious union with the universe in which the universe is seeking to see itself through our eyes while we are striving to understand the universe through universal eyes. If this wild proposition is true, then we might dare to ask what the universe is trying to learn through us at the same time as we are trying to make sense of the universe. Somewhere in this back-and forth we may be fortunate to experience the sort of mystical union, the *Unus mundus* Jung wrote of in a book titled *Mysterium Coniunctionis*. When humanity meets on fields that abut this domain, we discover that we share more in common than not. It is fitting to end on such a hopeful note since *The Map of the Soul* series was inspired by the enormously popular Korean musical group *BTS*, whose music, lyrics, and popularity seem to have tapped into many universal themes.

Endnotes

[1] Jung, CW Vol9/11 par. 3.
[2] Jung, CW Vol 9/11 par. 11.
[3] Jung, CW Vol 9/11 par. 18.

CPSIA information can be obtained
at www.ICGtesting.com
Printed in the USA
BVHW082027010622
638641BV00005B/1060